THE
PRESTIZIA PROTECTION PLAYBOOK

Real Stories. Real Protection.
Real Business Insurance.

9 Essential Coverages • 27 War Stories
• 28 Years of Experience

By John Crist, CPBL

President, Prestizia Insurance

Where Prestige Meets Strategy

Paperback ISBN: 978-1-961202-72-6
eBook ISBN: 978-1-961202-73-3

TABLE OF CONTENTS

Each chapter contains real-world stories from
28 years of insurance experience.

ABOUT THE AUTHOR

Twenty-eight years ago, I stepped into the world of insurance not because it was glamorous, but because it was needed. I saw good people—business owners, families, hardworking professionals—one unexpected event away from losing everything they'd worked for. I knew I could make a difference by helping them protect what mattered most.

That calling never left me.

In 2016, I founded Prestizia Insurance—a name built from Prestige + Strategy. The vision was simple: create an agency that combines excellence with thoughtful, long-term protection. Not price shopping. Not guesswork. But real strategy rooted in integrity.

Today, Prestizia Insurance proudly serves clients across AL, AR, FL, GA, ID, IL, KY, LA, MS, NC, OH, OK, SC, TN, and TX.

I am committed to guiding businesses, families, and corporations through the complex world of insurance with clarity, honesty, and expertise. I believe protection is not a product—it's a partnership.

Outside the office, I'm a husband, a father, a lifelong learner, and a proud member of the Dallas-Fort Worth community. I earned my Certified Professional Business Leader (CPBL) designation in 2025.

Every chapter of my journey comes back to one purpose:

"My mission is to help businesses, families, and corporations transform their insurance and financial challenges into clarity, confidence, and long-term protection."

That mission drives everything I do. One client at a time. One family at a time. One business at a time.

Contact Information
Prestizia Insurance
Phone: 972-854-7784
Email: service@prestiziainsurance.com
Website: PrestiziaInsurance.com
The Protection Circle: TheProtectionCircle.com
Office Address:
   6060 N Central Expy, Ste 500,
   Dallas, TX 75206
Social Media: @GoPrestizia (Instagram, Facebook, Twitter/X, TikTok, YouTube)

Chapter 1

GENERAL LIABILITY INSURANCE

*"The Policy Every Business Needs
Before They Open the Doors"*

If I could only recommend one insurance policy to a business owner who's just starting out, it would be General Liability insurance.

It's the foundation of any business insurance program. It protects you from the everyday risks that come with running a business—customer injuries, property damage, lawsuits from accidents that happen on your premises or because of your operations.

In my 28 years, I've seen General Liability save businesses from bankruptcy, and I've watched businesses without it close their doors because one lawsuit destroyed everything they built.

Let me show you what I mean with three real stories.

When General Liability Coverage SAVED a Business:

*"The Slip That Almost
Shut Down a Restaurant"*

A small family restaurant—one of those neighborhood spots where everyone knows your name—had been in business for 15 years without a single major incident.

Until one rainy Tuesday afternoon when a customer slipped on a wet floor near the entrance, fractured her hip, and ended up in surgery.

The medical bills came to $47,000. Then came the lawsuit for pain and suffering, lost wages, and permanent injury. The total demand? $340,000.

The restaurant owner was terrified. This wasn't a chain with deep pockets. This was a mom-and-pop operation running on thin margins. A $340,000 judgment would have meant bankruptcy, selling the building, and shutting down.

But they had General Liability insurance.

Here's what happened:
- ✓ The insurance company assigned a defense attorney
- ✓ All legal fees were covered (which ran over $65,000)
- ✓ The case went to mediation
- ✓ The insurance company negotiated a $180,000 settlement
- ✓ The policy paid every penny

The restaurant owner paid nothing out of pocket. The business stayed open. The employees kept their jobs. And the family didn't lose their livelihood.

That's what General Liability does—it turns a business-ending catastrophe into a manageable claim.

What General Liability Insurance Actually Covers

General Liability (GL) insurance—sometimes called Commercial General Liability (CGL)—is the broadest liability coverage a business can buy.

It typically covers four main areas:

1. Bodily Injury

   If someone gets hurt on your property or because of your business operations, GL covers their medical expenses, lost wages, and legal costs if they sue.

   Examples:
   - Customer slips and falls in your store
   - Client trips over equipment at a job site
   - Visitor injured by falling merchandise

2. Property Damage

   If your business damages someone else's property, GL covers the repair or replacement costs and any resulting lawsuits.

   Examples:
   - Your employee accidentally damages a client's building during work
   - Your equipment causes a fire in a rented space
   - You break a customer's expensive equipment while servicing it

3. Personal and Advertising Injury

   This covers claims of libel, slander, copyright infringement, or false advertising.

Examples:
- Competitor claims your ad copied their slogan
- Customer sues for defamation over a negative online response
- Copyright infringement claim over marketing materials

4. Medical Payments
   Covers minor medical expenses for injuries that occur on your premises, regardless of fault. This often prevents small incidents from becoming lawsuits.
   Typical limits: $5,000-$10,000 per person

When Someone DIDN'T Have General Liability:

"The Handyman Who Lost Everything"

A skilled handyman—great reputation, 10 years of satisfied customers—was working on a bathroom remodel. While installing a new vanity, he accidentally cracked a water line. Minor issue, right?

Wrong.

The leak went unnoticed for hours. By the time the homeowner discovered it, water had flooded through two floors, destroyed hardwood flooring, ruined drywall, and damaged furniture and electronics.

Total damage: $87,000.

The homeowner's insurance paid the claim—and then came after the handyman for reimbursement in a process called "subrogation."

The handyman had no General Liability insurance.

He had to pay:
- ✗ $87,000 in damages
- ✗ $12,000 in legal fees to defend himself
- ✗ Court costs

He drained his savings, maxed out credit cards, and eventually filed for bankruptcy. His business never recovered.

His exact words to me: "I thought I was being careful. I thought insurance was just an expense I could skip."

One mistake. One accident. No insurance. Business over.

Common General Liability SURPRISE:

"The Exclusion That Shocked the Building Owner"

A commercial property owner rented out several units to small businesses. He carried General Liability insurance and assumed he was fully protected.

Then one of his tenants—a small café—had a grease fire that spread and caused $200,000 in damage to the building.

The building owner filed a claim under his General Liability policy, fully expecting coverage.

The claim was denied.

Why?

General Liability policies have a critical exclusion: they don't cover damage to property you OWN, RENT, or OCCUPY.

Damage to his own building wasn't covered by GL—that's what Property insurance is for.

He had to pay the $200,000 repair bill out of pocket because he misunderstood what his GL policy covered.

The lesson: General Liability is powerful, but it's not a catch-all. You need to understand the exclusions just as much as the coverage.

Who Needs General Liability Insurance?

Short answer: Every business.

If you interact with customers, clients, or the public in any way, you need General Liability insurance.

You especially need it if you:
- Have a physical location where customers visit
- Perform work at client locations
- Manufacture or sell products
- Rent or lease commercial space
- Host events or have people on your property
- Have contracts that require GL coverage

How Much General Liability Coverage Do You Need?
The most common GL policy limit is $1 million per occurrence / $2 million aggregate.

Here's what that means:
- Per Occurrence Limit: The maximum the policy will pay for a single claim or incident ($1 million)

- Aggregate Limit: The maximum the policy will pay for all claims during the policy period ($2 million)
- For many small businesses, $1M/$2M is adequate. But you may need higher limits if:
- You have high-value clients or contracts
- Your lease or contracts require higher limits
- You operate in high-risk industries (construction, manufacturing)
- You have significant assets to protect

What Does General Liability Insurance Cost?

GL insurance is surprisingly affordable for most businesses.

Typical costs for $1M/$2M coverage:

- Low-risk office businesses: $400-$800/year
- Retail stores: $500-$1,500/year
- Restaurants: $1,000-$3,000/year
- Contractors: $1,500-$5,000+/year

Pricing factors:

- Your industry and risk level
- Annual revenue
- Number of employees
- Location
- Claims history
- Coverage limits

The Bottom Line

General Liability insurance is the single most important coverage for protecting your business from everyday risks.

It won't cover everything—you'll still need Property insurance, Workers Comp, Professional Liability, and other coverages depending on your business. But GL is where you start.

If you only buy one insurance policy, make it General Liability. Because one lawsuit, one accident, one injury can end everything you've worked for—and GL is the only thing standing between you and financial ruin.

Chapter 2
PROPERTY INSURANCE

"Protecting Your Physical Assets and Business Income"

Commercial Property insurance is one of those coverages that business owners understand conceptually but underestimate practically. Everyone knows their building and equipment need protection. What they don't always realize is that property insurance isn't just about replacing what burned down or got stolen—it's about keeping your business alive while you rebuild.

In my 28 years, I've seen property insurance save businesses that should have gone under, and I've watched underinsured owners learn expensive lessons they'll never forget.

Let me start with a story that shows what this coverage can really do when it's done right.

When Property Insurance—Especially Business Interruption—Saved a Business:

"The Diner That Burned at Midnight but Reopened at Dawn"

A mom-and-pop diner—the kind with bacon sizzling at 5 a.m. and customers who've sat in the same booth for

20 years—had an electrical fire in the kitchen. The flames didn't just scorch the walls... they shut the place down for seven full months.

The owners thought they were done. Payroll? Impossible. Rent? Still due. Suppliers? Still calling.

But here's where their policy became the quiet hero:
- ✓ Property coverage rebuilt the kitchen from the studs out
- ✓ Business Interruption kicked in like a lifeline— paying lost income, payroll, rent, and ongoing bills

One of the cooks said, "Man, this policy treated us better than some of our customers."

They reopened with the same staff, same menu, same regulars—because their insurance didn't just pay claims, it preserved their livelihood.

Moral: You don't buy insurance for buildings. You buy it for continuity.

What Property Insurance Actually Covers

Commercial Property insurance protects the physical assets of your business—the tangible things that allow you to operate.

It typically covers:
- Building (if you own it)
- Leasehold improvements (if you rent)
- Equipment and machinery
- Inventory and stock

- Furniture and fixtures
- Computers and electronics
- Signs (with proper endorsement)

Against these perils:
- Fire and smoke damage
- Theft and vandalism
- Wind and hail damage
- Water damage (from burst pipes, not flooding)
- Explosion

Critical component: Business Interruption (Business Income) Coverage

This is often the most valuable part of a property policy. It covers your lost income and continuing expenses when your business is forced to close due to a covered property loss.

Business Interruption pays for:
- Lost revenue during closure
- Payroll
- Rent or mortgage payments
- Utilities
- Loan payments
- Taxes

When Someone Was UNDERINSURED:

"The Coinsurance Clause That
Cost a Business Owner $110,000"

A small manufacturing shop had property insurance for $300,000. The owner thought that was plenty—his building and equipment were only worth about $400,000 at the time he bought the policy.

Five years later, the business had grown. New equipment. More inventory. Building improvements.

Then came the fire. $150,000 in damage. Not catastrophic, but significant.

He filed a claim, expecting a $150,000 payout.

He got $82,000.

What happened?

The Coinsurance Penalty.

Most property policies have an 80% coinsurance clause. This means you're required to insure your property for at least 80% of its full replacement value.

His property was now worth $600,000. He should have been insured for at least $480,000 (80%). But he was only carrying $300,000.

Because he was underinsured, the insurance company applied a coinsurance penalty formula:

- *(Amount of Insurance Carried ÷ Amount Required) × Loss = Payment*
- ($300,000 ÷ $480,000) × $150,000 = $93,750
- Minus his $10,000 deductible = $83,750 payout
- He had to pay the remaining $66,250 out of pocket.

Moral: It's not enough to have property insurance— you have to have ENOUGH property insurance. And 'enough' changes as your business grows.

Common Property Insurance SURPRISE:

"The Home-Based Business That Wasn't Covered"

A graphic designer ran her business from a dedicated home office. High-end computer equipment, servers, printers, client files—everything she needed to operate.

She had a standard homeowners insurance policy and assumed her business equipment was covered.

Then came the house fire.

Smoke. Fire. Water damage. All her business materials and inventory were gone.

She filed a homeowners claim fully expecting to be made whole.

Then the adjuster delivered the shocker.

Homeowners policies typically exclude or severely limit business property—often capped at something like $2,500.

She looked at the payout check like it was Monopoly money.

She never bought a BOP, never added a rider, never asked her agent. She assumed "home" meant "covered."

It didn't.

Moral: If business lives under your roof, make sure your policy knows about it—before the fire does.

What Property Insurance Typically Does NOT Cover

Understanding exclusions is just as important as understanding coverage.

Common exclusions:
- Flood damage (requires separate flood insurance)
- Earthquake damage (requires separate earthquake coverage)
- Mold (often excluded or limited)
- Wear and tear or deterioration
- Mechanical breakdown (covered under Equipment Breakdown coverage)
- Employee theft (covered under Crime insurance)
- Outdoor property (trees, fences—may require endorsement)

How Much Property Coverage Do You Need?
Rule: Insure to 100% replacement cost, not actual cash value.

- Replacement Cost: Pays to rebuild or replace property with new materials at current prices
- Actual Cash Value: Pays replacement cost minus depreciation (often leaves you significantly short)

Recommendation: Get a professional appraisal every 3-5 years

Construction costs, equipment values, and inventory levels change. Your coverage should too.

The Bottom Line
Property insurance is about more than protecting your stuff. It's about protecting your ability to keep operating when disaster strikes.

The diner that reopened after the fire? Business Interruption coverage kept them alive. The manufacturer who got hit with coinsurance? He learned the hard way that 'having insurance' isn't the same as 'having enough insurance.' The home-based business owner? She discovered that assumptions cost money.

Don't make those mistakes. Insure your property to full replacement value, include Business Interruption, and review your coverage every year as your business grows.

Chapter 3

COMMERCIAL AUTO INSURANCE

"When Your Business Uses Vehicles"

If your business involves vehicles—company trucks, delivery vans, employees running errands, or even just someone grabbing supplies in their personal car—you need Commercial Auto insurance. Not maybe. Not eventually. Now.

I've seen too many business owners assume their personal auto insurance covers business use. It doesn't. I've watched businesses get blindsided by claims they thought were covered. And I've seen one accident nearly bankrupt a company because they didn't have the right coverage in place.

But I've also seen Commercial Auto policies save businesses when disaster struck. Let me show you what I mean.

When Commercial Auto Coverage SAVED a Business:

"The Delivery Van That Hit the Worst Day of Its Life—and the Business Still Survived"

A small HVAC company had a work van out on a routine service call. Their tech—good guy, reliable, never had an accident in 12 years—got T-boned by a driver who ran a red light.

The van spun, hit a pole, and the equipment in the back turned into flying metal. Two cars were damaged. One driver went to the hospital. The tech needed surgery. The van was totaled. And three customers were expecting installs that same day.

It looked like a domino line headed straight for disaster.

But here's where their Commercial Auto policy stood tall:
- ✓ Liability coverage took care of the injured driver, damaged vehicles, legal fees, and settlements.
- ✓ Collision coverage replaced the totaled van.
- ✓ Medical payments helped the tech through recovery.
- ✓ Rental reimbursement kept the business operating until the new van arrived.
- ✓ Coverage for tools/equipment replaced what was destroyed in the crash.

The owner said, "If that policy wasn't there, one accident would've become our obituary."

Instead, they kept every job, every employee, and rolled on like the pros they were.

Moral: One bad day can happen to anyone—but one good policy can save everything.

What Commercial Auto Insurance Actually Covers

Commercial Auto insurance protects your business when vehicles are used for business purposes. Whether you own a fleet of trucks or occasionally send employees on errands, this coverage is critical.

Here's what it typically covers:

- Liability Coverage—Pays for bodily injury and property damage your vehicle causes to others. If your employee causes an accident, this covers the other party's medical bills, vehicle repairs, lost wages, and legal fees if you're sued. This is required by law in most states.
- Collision Coverage—Pays to repair or replace your vehicle if it's damaged in an accident, regardless of who's at fault. Your van hits a pole? Collision covers it. Another vehicle hits you? Collision covers it.
- Comprehensive Coverage—Covers damage to your vehicle from non-collision events: theft, vandalism, fire, hail, hitting a deer, falling objects, and natural disasters. Basically, if it's not a collision with another vehicle or object, comprehensive handles it.
- Medical Payments Coverage—Pays medical expenses for you and your passengers after an accident, regardless of fault. This provides immediate medical coverage without waiting to determine liability.
- Uninsured/Underinsured Motorist Coverage— Protects you when the at-fault driver has no insurance or not enough insurance to cover your damages. This is more common than you'd think.
- Rental Reimbursement—Pays for a rental vehicle while your vehicle is being repaired after a covered

loss. This keeps your business operating without interruption.

- Towing and Labor—Covers the cost of towing your vehicle to a repair shop and roadside assistance.
- Tools and Equipment Coverage—Covers tools, equipment, and materials in your vehicle if they're damaged or stolen. Standard auto policies don't cover this, but it's critical for contractors, technicians, and service businesses.

What Commercial Auto Insurance Does NOT Cover (And the Gaps That Hurt)

Here's where business owners get caught:

- Personal use of commercial vehicles—If your employee takes the work truck to run personal errands and causes an accident, coverage may be denied or limited depending on your policy.
- Employees using personal vehicles for business—This is the big one. If your employee uses their personal car for business errands, their personal auto insurance will likely deny the claim. You need Hired and Non-Owned Auto coverage for this.
- Rideshare and delivery apps—If your employee is driving for Uber, Lyft, DoorDash, or other gig economy platforms using a company vehicle, standard commercial policies exclude this. They need specialized rideshare/delivery coverage.
- Cargo/freight in transit—If you're transporting goods for hire, you need separate cargo insurance.

Commercial auto doesn't cover the value of what you're hauling for clients.

- Trailers and attached equipment—These often need to be specifically scheduled on your policy.

Let me show you what happens when businesses don't understand these gaps.

When Someone Had a GAP in Auto Coverage:

"The Employee Errand That Cost the Business $38,000"

A bakery sent one of their employees to pick up supplies in her personal car—something she'd done a dozen times before.

On the way back, she rear-ended a luxury SUV. No injuries, but the SUV's repair estimate could've fed a village.

The owner called in the claim expecting the employee's personal auto insurance to handle things.

Then the surprise hit:

  ✗ Personal auto policies deny coverage when the vehicle is being used for business.

  ✗ The bakery didn't have Hired & Non-Owned Auto on their commercial policy.

That meant the business was fully responsible. Every dollar. Every repair. Every headache.

The check they wrote to fix that SUV was more than their oven cost. And it nearly burned their entire month's profits.

Moral: If employees ever drive for you—even "just to grab something real quick"—you need Hired & Non-Owned Auto.

Hired and Non-Owned Auto Coverage: The Coverage Every Business Needs

This is one of the most misunderstood—and most critical—coverages for businesses.

Hired Auto Coverage—Protects your business when you rent or lease vehicles for business use. Company car rental? Rented moving truck? This covers it.

Non-Owned Auto Coverage—Protects your business when employees use their personal vehicles for business purposes. Employee runs to the bank in their car? Drives to a client meeting? Picks up supplies? This coverage responds if they cause an accident.

Why You Need This:

When an employee uses their personal vehicle for business and causes an accident:

1. Their personal auto insurance denies the claim (business use exclusion)
2. The injured party sues your business (you directed the employee to drive)
3. Without Hired & Non-Owned coverage, you pay out of pocket

The good news? Hired and Non-Owned Auto coverage is incredibly affordable—typically $200-500 per year. The bad news? Most businesses don't have it until they need it.

Who needs it:

- Any business where employees occasionally drive their personal vehicles for business

- Businesses that rent vehicles for business purposes
- Businesses with sales reps, delivery staff, or mobile employees
- Basically, every business

Personal vs. Commercial Auto: When You Need Commercial

Many business owners wonder if they can just use their personal auto insurance for business vehicles. The answer is almost always no.

You need Commercial Auto insurance if:

✓ The vehicle is owned or leased by the business
✓ The vehicle has business logos, wraps, or signage
✓ The vehicle is used primarily for business purposes
✓ The vehicle is a commercial type (box truck, cargo van, dump truck)
✓ The vehicle carries tools, equipment, or inventory
✓ The vehicle is used to transport clients or goods for hire
✓ You have multiple vehicles

Personal auto insurance is for:

- Commuting to and from work
- Personal errands and activities
- Occasional business use (very limited)

The line gets blurry when employees use personal vehicles occasionally for business. That's why Hired and Non-Owned coverage exists.

Let me show you what happens when businesses blur this line without proper coverage.

Common Commercial Auto SURPRISE:

*"The Landscaping Crew and the Logo
That Changed Everything"*

A landscaping company decided to upgrade their brand by putting their new logo on all their trucks. They looked sharp—professional, unified, ready for business.

But no one told the insurance carrier.

A month later, a crew member backed a truck into a customer's garage door. The owner filed a claim... and the adjuster delivered the unexpected:

When you place a business logo or wrap on a vehicle, most states consider it a commercial vehicle—even if it's registered personally.

And a personal auto policy can deny coverage for vehicles used to generate business income.

Result?

X Personal auto carrier refused the claim.
X The business had no Commercial Auto policy.
X They paid for:
- Garage repairs
- Truck repairs
- Lost tools
- The deductible on the homeowner's policy (yes, they had to reimburse it)

The owner said, "I didn't know a sticker could cost me five grand."

Moral: If the vehicle promotes your business or profits your business—insure it as a business vehicle.

How Commercial Auto Premiums Are Calculated

Commercial auto insurance costs more than personal auto because the risk is higher. Vehicles used for business typically:

- Drive more miles
- Operate in different conditions
- Carry valuable equipment or cargo
- Are driven by multiple people

Factors that affect your premium:

- Type of vehicle—A delivery van costs more than a sedan
- Vehicle value—Higher value = higher premium
- How the vehicle is used—Local delivery vs. long-haul vs. service calls
- Radius of operation—Local (within 50 miles) vs. regional vs. nationwide
- Cargo/equipment value—What you're carrying
- Number of vehicles—Fleets may get volume discounts
- Driver records—MVR (motor vehicle record) of all drivers matters
- Annual mileage—More miles = more risk
- Business type—A florist faces different risks than a roofing contractor
- Coverage limits—Higher limits = higher premium
- Deductibles—Higher deductibles = lower premium

Real Costs: What You'll Actually Pay

Here are ballpark figures for commercial auto insurance:
- Single vehicle (light commercial use): $1,200-2,500/ year
- Cargo van or pickup truck: $1,500-3,500/year
- Box truck or larger vehicle: $3,000-7,000/year
- Fleet (5+ vehicles): $1,000-2,500/vehicle/year (volume discounts apply)
- Hired & Non-Owned Auto only: $200-500/year

These are estimates. Your actual cost depends on all the factors above.

Coverage Limits: How Much Do You Need?

Most states require minimum liability limits for commercial vehicles, but these minimums are rarely enough. A serious accident can easily exceed state minimums.

Common liability limit structures:
- State minimum—Often $25,000/$50,000/$25,000 (Not recommended)
- Standard—$500,000 combined single limit
- Recommended—$1,000,000 combined single limit
- High-risk or large fleet—$2,000,000+ or add Commercial Umbrella

If you own the vehicle, add:
- Collision coverage (with deductible of $500-1,000)
- Comprehensive coverage (with deductible of $500-1,000)

- Rental reimbursement
- Tools and equipment coverage (if applicable)

When to Buy Commercial Auto Insurance

The answer is simple: Before the vehicle is used for business.

You need coverage in place:
- Before taking delivery of a company vehicle
- Before an employee makes their first business-related drive
- Before you add logos or business signage to any vehicle
- Before you rent a vehicle for business purposes

Don't wait. One accident without coverage can end your business.

Fleet Management and Loss Control

If you have multiple vehicles, implement these practices to reduce risk and lower premiums:

1. Driver qualification program
   - Check MVRs before hiring
   - Establish minimum standards (no major violations, etc.)
   - Re-check MVRs annually
2. Written vehicle use policy
   - Define acceptable use
   - Prohibit distractions (cell phones, eating, etc.)
   - Require seat belts
   - Set consequences for violations

3. Driver training
   - Defensive driving courses
   - Vehicle-specific training
   - Regular safety meetings
4. Vehicle maintenance
   - Regular inspections
   - Documented maintenance schedules
   - Replace worn tires immediately
5. Telematics/GPS tracking
   - Monitor driver behavior
   - Identify unsafe patterns
   - Improve route efficiency

Insurers often offer discounts for formal safety programs.

The Bottom Line

Commercial Auto insurance protects your business when vehicles are involved. Whether you own a fleet or occasionally send employees on errands, you need proper coverage.

Don't assume personal auto policies cover business use. They don't.

Don't skip Hired and Non-Owned coverage. It's cheap, and the first time you need it, you'll be grateful it's there.

And please—if you put your business name on a vehicle, insure it as a business vehicle.

Next Steps:

1. List all vehicles used for business (owned, leased, or employee-owned)

2. Verify you have Commercial Auto coverage for company vehicles
3. Add Hired and Non-Owned Auto coverage if employees ever drive for business
4. Review your coverage limits—state minimums aren't enough
5. Remove business logos from personally-insured vehicles or switch to commercial coverage
6. Implement a driver safety program if you have multiple vehicles

Key Takeaway: One accident involving a business vehicle can cost hundreds of thousands of dollars. Commercial Auto insurance ensures that one bad day doesn't become your last day in business.

Chapter 4

WORKERS COMPENSATION INSURANCE

"Required by Law, Critical for Protection"

Workers Compensation insurance is different from every other coverage we've discussed. It's not optional. It's not a "nice to have." In most states, if you have employees, you must carry Workers Compensation insurance. It's the law.

But beyond the legal requirement, Workers Comp serves a critical purpose: it protects both your employees and your business when someone gets hurt on the job. Without it, a single workplace injury can bankrupt your company and ruin an employee's life.

In my 28 years, I've seen Workers Comp policies save businesses from financial ruin and employees from devastating medical debt. I've also watched businesses without coverage collapse under the weight of a single injury.

Let me show you why this coverage matters so much.

When Workers' Comp SAVED a Business (and an Employee):

"The Warehouse Fall That Could've Broken Everything—Except They Had Coverage"

A distribution warehouse had a long-time employee, solid worker, dependable as sunrise. One afternoon he slipped off a loading ramp while guiding a pallet jack and went down hard. Broken leg. Torn ligaments. Surgery needed. Months of physical therapy.

In that split second, the owner's mind ran wild: medical bills... wage replacement... lawsuits... shutting down...

But this time, the policy was the hero standing in the wings.

- ✓ Workers' Comp paid every medical bill—surgery, rehab, medication, follow-ups.
- ✓ Paid his lost wages while he healed, so his family didn't miss rent or groceries.
- ✓ Protected the business from lawsuits, because WC is the exclusive remedy.
- ✓ Brought him back to work—stronger, loyal, grateful.

The owner said, "That policy didn't just save my business... it saved my relationship with a man who helped build it."

Moral: One injury can break bones—or it can break a business. Workers' Comp decides which one.

What Workers Compensation Insurance Actually Covers

Workers Compensation is a no-fault insurance system designed to provide benefits to employees injured on the job, while protecting employers from lawsuits. Here's what it covers:

- Medical Expenses—All reasonable and necessary medical treatment related to the work injury:

emergency care, hospital stays, surgery, prescription medications, physical therapy, medical equipment, and ongoing treatment. There are no deductibles and no co-pays for the employee.

- Lost Wages—Typically pays about two-thirds of the employee's average weekly wage while they're unable to work due to the injury. Benefits usually start after a waiting period (3-7 days depending on the state). If the disability extends beyond a certain period, benefits are often paid retroactively from day one.

- Permanent Disability Benefits—If the injury results in permanent impairment, the employee receives compensation based on the severity and type of disability. This could be partial or total, temporary or permanent.

- Vocational Rehabilitation—If an employee can't return to their previous job due to the injury, Workers Comp may pay for retraining or job placement services.

- Death Benefits—If an employee dies from a work-related injury or illness, Workers Comp provides burial expenses and ongoing benefits to surviving dependents.

- The Exclusive Remedy Provision—This is the crucial trade-off: employees receive guaranteed benefits regardless of fault, and in exchange, they give up the right to sue their employer for the injury (with very limited exceptions for gross negligence or intentional harm).

Why Workers Compensation is Legally Required

Workers Compensation laws exist in all 50 states, though requirements vary by state. Most states require coverage as soon as you hire your first employee, but some have thresholds based on number of employees or industry.

Typical requirements:
- Most states: 1 or more employees
- Some states: 3-5 employees depending on industry
- Certain high-risk industries: Required even for sole proprietors
- Agriculture, construction, domestic workers: Special rules apply

Penalties for not having Workers Comp when required:
- Significant fines (often $1,000+ per day without coverage)
- Criminal penalties in some states
- Personal liability for employee injuries
- Stop-work orders shutting down your business
- Inability to bid on contracts or obtain licenses

But beyond legal compliance, there's a bigger reason to carry Workers Comp: one serious injury can destroy your business financially if you don't have coverage.

Let me show you what happens when business owners try to operate without it.

When Someone Had a GAP or NO Workers' Comp at All:

"The 'We're Too Small' Myth That Cost a Business Its Future"

A small cleaning company had three workers. The owner insisted they were "1099 contractors," even though he controlled the schedule, provided the supplies, and paid them hourly.

One day, one of the cleaners fell down a flight of stairs at a client's office building and tore her back up badly. Couldn't work. Needed imaging, therapy, and time off.

He thought her personal insurance would handle it.

Then the avalanche hit:
- ✗ She wasn't a true contractor under state law—she was an employee.
- ✗ No Workers' Comp policy in place.
- ✗ She filed a lawsuit for medical costs, lost wages, and negligence.
- ✗ The business paid tens of thousands out of pocket, plus attorney fees.
- ✗ Lost the contract with the building.

Six months later, he shut the company down.

All because he thought Workers' Comp was "only for big businesses."

Moral: If someone works like an employee, moves like an employee, and depends on your business—the state calls them an employee whether you like it or not.

The 1099 Contractor Myth

This is one of the most dangerous misconceptions in business: "If I pay people as 1099 contractors, I don't need Workers Comp."

Wrong.

States use specific tests to determine if someone is truly an independent contractor or actually an employee. Simply calling someone a 1099 contractor doesn't make it so.

Common tests states use:

- Control Test—Who controls how, when, and where the work is done? If you control the details, they're likely an employee.
- Economic Reality Test—Is the worker economically dependent on your business, or do they operate their own independent business?

ABC Test (used in many states):

- A: Worker is free from control and direction
- B: Work is outside the usual course of your business
- C: Worker is customarily engaged in an independently established trade

Red flags that scream "employee, not contractor":

- You set their schedule
- You provide tools, equipment, or supplies
- They work only for you
- You train them how to do the work
- You pay them hourly or salary (not per project)
- They don't have their own business entity

- They can't hire their own helpers

What happens if you misclassify:
- State orders you to provide Workers Comp coverage retroactively
- You pay back premiums for all misclassified workers
- Penalties and fines stack up
- If a worker gets injured, you're personally liable
- IRS may come after you for payroll taxes too

The safe approach: If you're not sure, assume they're an employee and get Workers Comp coverage. It's cheaper than the alternative.

How Workers Compensation Premiums Are Calculated

Workers Comp premiums aren't random. They're calculated using a specific formula based on your payroll, industry risk, and claims history.

The Formula:
- (Payroll / $100) × Class Code Rate × Experience Modification Factor = Premium

Let me break that down:
- Payroll—Your total employee payroll (excluding owners in some cases). Every $100 of payroll is a unit of exposure.
- Class Code Rate—Each job type has a classification code with an assigned rate per $100 of payroll. Rates vary wildly by risk level.

Examples of class codes and rates (per $100 of payroll):
- Office clerical: $0.20-0.50
- Restaurant server: $1.50-3.00
- Retail sales: $0.80-2.00
- Construction carpenter: $8.00-15.00
- Roofing: $15.00-40.00+

A roofer pays 50-100 times more than an office worker because the risk is dramatically higher.

Experience Modification Factor (Mod)—This is your company's claims history compared to others in your industry. It starts at 1.00 (average). If you have fewer claims than expected, your mod drops below 1.00, reducing your premium. If you have more claims, your mod goes above 1.00, increasing your premium.

Example:
- Clean record for 3 years: Mod drops to 0.85 (15% discount)
- Multiple claims: Mod rises to 1.25 (25% surcharge)

Your experience mod can make or break your premium. One serious claim can impact your rates for 3-5 years.

The Workers Comp Audit

Here's something that surprises business owners: Workers Comp policies are audited annually.

When you buy the policy, the premium is estimated based on projected payroll. At the end of the policy term, the insurance company audits your actual payroll and adjusts the premium accordingly.

If your actual payroll was higher than estimated, you owe more. If it was lower, you get a refund.

What the auditor looks for:
- Actual payroll records
- 1099 forms for contractors
- Certificates of insurance from subcontractors
- Officer/owner payroll
- Employee job classifications
- Overtime pay
- Tips, bonuses, and commissions

Where business owners get caught:

Let me show you.

Common Workers' Comp SURPRISE:

"The Audit That Turned a Small
Mistake Into a Costly Lesson"

A contractor hired "temporary help" during their busy season—a couple of part-timers and a supervisor who "only worked weekends." He didn't report the payroll because he figured the jobs were short-term, and he assumed they didn't need to be listed.

Then came the annual Workers' Comp audit.

The auditor asked for payroll records, 1099s, check stubs... and discovered:
- X Unreported payroll
- X Misclassified workers

X A supervisor doing high-risk tasks but listed as clerical

X A subcontractor with no WC certificate—meaning the contractor was now responsible

The bill for the additional premium and penalties? $22,000.

The owner said, "I didn't think they actually looked at all that."

The auditor said, "Sir, that's literally my entire job."

Moral: Workers' Comp isn't just a premium—it's a math equation. Skip a line, and the bill writes itself later.

Subcontractors and Certificates of Insurance

If you hire subcontractors, you must obtain proof that they carry their own Workers Comp insurance. If they don't have coverage, you become responsible for their workers.

What you need:
- Certificate of Insurance showing active Workers Comp coverage
- Coverage dates that match when they're working for you
- Verification that it's actually in force

What happens if you don't get certificates:

During the audit, the insurance company will assume all subcontractor payments are actually your employees. They'll add those payments to your payroll and charge you the premium.

If your sub paid out $50,000 to their workers and has a high-risk classification code, you could suddenly owe $5,000-10,000 in additional premium.

Best practice: Before any sub starts work, get their certificate. Keep a file. Update it annually. No exceptions.

Real Costs: What You'll Actually Pay
Workers Comp premiums vary dramatically by industry. Here are ballpark costs:

Low-risk industries:
- Office/clerical work: $500-1,500/year per $100K payroll
- Retail stores: $1,000-3,000/year per $100K payroll
- Restaurants: $2,000-5,000/year per $100K payroll

Medium-risk industries:
- Landscaping: $3,000-8,000/year per $100K payroll
- Plumbing: $5,000-10,000/year per $100K payroll
- HVAC: $5,000-12,000/year per $100K payroll

High-risk industries:
- Roofing: $15,000-40,000/year per $100K payroll
- Tree services: $20,000-50,000/year per $100K payroll
- Demolition: $25,000-60,000/year per $100K payroll

Your actual cost depends on your specific class codes, payroll, claims history, and state.

Controlling Your Workers Comp Costs
Workers Comp premiums can be one of your largest insurance expenses, especially in high-risk industries. Here's how to keep costs down:

1. Implement a Safety Program
   - Formal written safety policies
   - Regular safety training
   - PPE (personal protective equipment) requirements
   - Pre-job safety meetings
   - Hazard identification and correction
2. Return-to-Work Programs
   - Light duty or modified work for injured employees
   - Gets employees back to work faster
   - Reduces lost-time claims
   - Shows you care about your people
3. Manage Claims Aggressively
   - Report injuries immediately
   - Work with injured employees
   - Stay in contact during recovery
   - Challenge fraudulent claims
   - Use approved medical providers
4. Audit Your Payroll Classifications
   - Make sure employees are in the correct class codes
   - Don't let everyone default to the highest-risk code
   - Review classifications at each renewal
5. Shop Your Coverage
   - Get quotes from multiple carriers every 2-3 years
   - Rates and appetite vary by carrier
   - Some specialize in specific industries
6. Improve Your Experience Mod
   - Few or no claims = lower mod = lower premium

- One bad year affects your mod for 3 years
- Focus on prevention, not just treatment

When to Buy Workers Compensation Insurance

The answer is simple: Before your first employee starts work.

Not after they start. Not "once we get a few employees." Before day one.

Many states impose severe penalties for operating even one day without required coverage. And if an injury happens on that employee's first day, you're personally liable for all costs.

You need Workers Comp before:
- Your first employee's first day
- Hiring seasonal or temporary workers
- Bringing on part-time help
- Starting construction on a project
- Opening for business

The Bottom Line

Workers Compensation insurance isn't optional. It's required by law in most states, and for good reason. Workplace injuries happen, and when they do, Workers Comp protects both your employees and your business.

Don't try to save money by calling employees "contractors" if they're not truly independent. Don't skip coverage because you're small. Don't hide payroll from auditors.

One serious injury without coverage can bankrupt your business and leave an injured worker with no help. That's not a risk worth taking.

Get the coverage. Pay your premiums. Implement safety programs. Treat your employees well. And if someone gets hurt, handle it properly.

Next Steps:

1. Verify you have Workers Comp coverage if you have employees
2. Get certificates of insurance from all subcontractors before they work
3. Review your payroll classifications to ensure accuracy
4. Implement a written safety program
5. Create a return-to-work policy for injured employees
6. Keep detailed payroll records for audit purposes
7. Shop your coverage every 2-3 years to ensure competitive rates

Key Takeaway: Workers Compensation protects your employees when they're injured and protects your business from financial catastrophe. It's required by law, but more importantly, it's the right thing to do.

Chapter 5

PROFESSIONAL LIABILITY (E&O) INSURANCE

"When Your Expertise Becomes Your Exposure"

If you make a living from advice, expertise, or professional services, you're operating in a world where mistakes don't just cost reputation—they cost lawsuits.

Professional Liability insurance—often called Errors & Omissions (E&O) coverage—is the only thing standing between a service professional and financial ruin when a client decides that your work, your advice, or your oversight caused them harm.

In my 28 years, I've seen E&O policies save careers, and I've watched professionals without coverage lose everything they built because of one angry client and one lawsuit.

Here's how it plays out in the real world.

When E&O Coverage SAVED a Business:

"The Consultant's Oversight That Should've Ended the Firm—But Didn't"

A business consultant advised a client on a workflow redesign that was supposed to cut costs. Instead, due to a missed regulatory requirement, the client ended up being fined nearly $140,000.

The client wasn't just upset—they were furious. Their attorney drafted a demand letter claiming negligence, financial damages, and breach of professional duty.

The consultant's stomach dropped. This was the kind of mistake that could shut down a small firm overnight.

But here's where the E&O policy stepped onto the battlefield:

- Defense counsel paid for
- All legal fees covered
- Negotiated settlement covered
- Consultant paid zero out-of-pocket
- Business kept operating without missing a beat

The consultant said afterward, "That E&O policy wasn't an expense—it was my second chance."

Moral: When your advice becomes someone else's loss, the lawsuit is coming. E&O is the only shield that holds.

What Professional Liability (E&O) Insurance Actually Covers

Professional Liability insurance protects you when your professional services—your advice, your work product, your expertise—are alleged to have caused financial harm to a client.

It typically covers:

- Negligence or errors in professional services
- Omissions—things you failed to do or advise

- Misrepresentation—incorrect advice or information
- Breach of professional duty
- Legal defense costs—even if the claim is groundless
- Settlements and judgments up to policy limits

It does NOT cover:
- Bodily injury or property damage (that's General Liability)
- Intentional wrongdoing or fraud
- Criminal acts
- Contractual disputes unrelated to professional services
- Employment-related claims (that's EPLI)

The tricky part? E&O is almost always written on a claims-made basis, not occurrence. That means the claim must be made during the policy period, not when the work was done. More on that nightmare scenario in Story #3.

When Someone Had a GAP or NO E&O at All:

*"The Accountant Who Thought Their
Reputation Was Coverage Enough"*

A small accountant handled bookkeeping for several boutiques. One year, she made a misclassification error that caused a client to underpay sales tax by over $20,000.

The notice came months later—with penalties and interest that pushed it near $35,000.

The client blamed her and demanded reimbursement. When she refused, they sued.

She had general liability, but no E&O. She said, "I've been doing this 15 years. I don't make mistakes."

The courts see it differently.

She had to pay:
- Her attorney retainer
- Court costs
- A chunk of the settlement
- Lost business from reputational damage

One lawsuit drained half her savings. She trimmed her client list, closed her office, and worked from home part-time.

Her final words about it were brutal and honest: "I thought I was saving $80 a month. Turns out I was gambling with everything I built."

Moral: Professional mistakes don't have to be big—but the fallout always is.

Common E&O SURPRISE:

"The Retroactive Date That Almost Cost a Tech Firm $90,000"

A small IT company switched carriers to save money. When they moved their E&O policy, they didn't notice the new policy's retroactive date reset to the date the policy started.

Two months later, a client discovered a coding error from work done three years earlier—well before the new policy's retro date.

They filed a claim for data loss and downtime. The IT company was confident they were covered.

Then came the gut punch:
- Claims-made policy
- Work occurred before the retro date
- Claim denied

Their old carrier wouldn't cover it because the claim was made after cancellation. Their new carrier wouldn't cover it because the error was before the retro date.

They were stuck in no-man's-land. They had to pay the $90,000 bill themselves.

The owner told his agent, "I didn't even know a retroactive date was a thing."

Moral: In E&O, the danger isn't what you see—it's what happened years ago that finally shows up.

Who Needs Professional Liability Insurance?
If you provide professional services, advice, or expertise for a fee, you need E&O. Period.

Industries that absolutely need it:
- Consultants (business, IT, HR, marketing)
- Accountants and bookkeepers
- Financial advisors and insurance agents
- Real estate agents and brokers
- Architects and engineers
- Attorneys
- Technology and software companies

- Medical professionals (often called Medical Malpractice)
- Marketing and advertising agencies
- Designers and creative professionals

The rule of thumb: If a client could sue you for making a mistake, giving bad advice, or failing to deliver what you promised, you need E&O.

Key Terms You Need to Understand

Claims-Made vs. Occurrence

Most E&O policies are claims-made, which means:
- The claim must be made while the policy is active
- Even if the work was done years ago, the claim date matters
- Occurrence policies cover incidents that happen during the policy period, regardless of when the claim is filed. These are rare in E&O.

Retroactive Date
- The earliest date for which coverage applies. Any work done before this date won't be covered, even if the claim is made during the policy period.

Critical: When you switch carriers, make sure your new policy's retroactive date matches your original coverage date, or you'll have a coverage gap.

Extended Reporting Period (Tail Coverage)
- If you cancel your claims-made policy, you can buy "tail coverage" that extends the reporting period for claims arising from work done while the policy was active.

This is expensive but essential if you're retiring, selling your business, or switching carriers without continuous coverage.

Prior Acts Coverage
- Coverage for work performed before the policy's effective date but after the retroactive date. Make sure this is included when switching carriers.

How Much E&O Coverage Do You Need?
Standard limits: $1 million per claim / $2 million aggregate is the baseline for most small professional firms.

You may need higher limits if:
- Your clients are large corporations
- Your contracts require specific minimum coverage
- Your advice directly impacts major financial decisions
- You operate in high-risk fields (finance, healthcare, legal)

Cost factors:
- Your profession (accountants pay less than attorneys)
- Your claims history
- Your revenue and number of employees
- Policy limits and deductible
- Typical costs range from $500-$3,000/year for small firms, but high-risk professions can pay significantly more.

The Bottom Line

You spent years building your expertise, your reputation, and your client base. One mistake—or even one alleged mistake—can wipe it all out if you're not protected.

E&O insurance isn't about admitting you're going to make mistakes. It's about acknowledging that in professional services, the difference between a happy client and a lawsuit is often razor-thin, and you need protection when perception doesn't match reality.

If you sell advice, expertise, or professional services, E&O isn't optional. It's survival.

Next up: Chapter 6 will cover Cyber Liability—because in 2025, data breaches aren't just an IT problem, they're a business-ending event.

Chapter 6

CYBER LIABILITY INSURANCE

"The Coverage That Didn't Exist 20 Years Ago—
But Today It's Life or Death"

When I started in insurance 28 years ago, Cyber Liability didn't exist. There was no such thing as ransomware, phishing scams, or data breach notifications. Businesses worried about fires and lawsuits—not hackers halfway around the world encrypting their files and demanding Bitcoin.

Today, cyber attacks aren't just an IT problem. They're an existential threat. A single email, one clicked link, one compromised password—and your entire business can be locked down, drained, or destroyed in hours.

And here's the scariest part: most business owners still think they're too small to be targeted, or that their general liability covers cyber incidents. Neither is true.

In my 28 years, I've watched Cyber Insurance go from 'optional add-on' to 'business survival tool.' Let me show you why.

When Cyber Insurance SAVED a Business:

"The Ransomware Attack That Locked the Whole Company—Until the Policy Became the Hero"

A small medical billing company came in one Monday and found every file encrypted. Invoices, patient info, contracts, payroll—locked behind a hacker's ransom note.

The attacker wanted $62,000 in cryptocurrency. The owner froze. No systems. No revenue. No access. Patients couldn't be billed. Providers couldn't be paid. Every day down meant thousands lost.

- But they had Cyber Insurance—and the cavalry rolled in fast.
- Forensics team identified the origin of the breach
- Legal counsel guided them on compliance
- Notification costs for affected patients were covered
- Credit monitoring was paid for
- Ransom negotiation team stepped in
- Business interruption coverage paid for the revenue they lost during downtime
- System restoration brought everything back online

They paid just the deductible. The policy handled the rest. In three weeks, they were fully operational—and survived what should've been a death sentence.

The owner said, "If I didn't have this policy, I'd be in bankruptcy court instead of my office."

Moral: When hackers shut your business down, Cyber Insurance is the only key that gets the doors open again.

What Cyber Liability Insurance Actually Covers

Cyber Liability insurance is designed to help businesses survive the financial devastation of a cyber attack or data breach.

Unlike traditional insurance that protects against physical damage, Cyber Insurance protects against digital threats—and the expensive aftermath that follows.

First-Party Coverage (costs YOU incur):
- Data breach response costs (forensics, legal counsel, notification, credit monitoring)
- Ransomware payments and negotiation
- Business interruption (lost income during system downtime)
- Data restoration and system recovery
- Crisis management and PR expenses
- Cyber extortion payments
- Regulatory fines and penalties (in some policies)

Third-Party Coverage (costs from OTHERS suing you):
- Legal defense costs if customers or clients sue you
- Settlements and judgments
- Regulatory defense costs (HIPAA, PCI-DSS, state privacy laws)
- Claims of failure to protect data

Optional (but CRITICAL) Add-Ons:
- Social engineering/funds transfer fraud (covers wire fraud from spoofed emails)
- Dependent business interruption (if a vendor's breach affects you)
- Crypto-jacking and crypto-currency theft
- Bricking (hardware damage from cyber attack)

It does NOT cover:
- Bodily injury or property damage (that's General Liability)
- Intellectual property theft (usually needs separate IP coverage)
- Betterment or upgrades to systems (only restores to pre-breach state)
- Prior known breaches or incidents

When Someone Had NO Cyber Coverage:

"The Boutique Firm That Thought 'We're Too Small'... Until a Hack Cleaned Them Out"

A small architectural firm with eight employees got hit by a phishing email pretending to be a vendor. An employee clicked a link, malware installed, and within hours the attackers had:
- Copied customer files
- Accessed project blueprints
- Locked their server
- Stole client credit card numbers
- Downloaded proprietary designs
- The fallout was brutal:
- $18,000 for forensic analysis
- $27,000 for client notification and credit monitoring
- $40,000 in lost business from system downtime
- $16,000 in legal fees
- One client threatened to sue for negligence
- They had a BOP and general liability, but neither covers cyber breaches.

They ended up draining their savings and maxing credit lines. The owner said the words no business owner ever wants to speak:

- "I didn't know cyber wasn't included. I learned the expensive way."
- They limped along another year before finally closing.

Moral: The only thing more expensive than Cyber Insurance... is not having Cyber Insurance.

Common Cyber Insurance SURPRISE:

"The Wire Fraud That Wasn't Covered—
and Shocked the Owner"

A real estate brokerage received an email that looked exactly like their title company: same signature, same tone, same transaction details.

Except it wasn't them.

A hacker had slipped into an employee's inbox, studied communication patterns, and sent perfectly spoofed payment instructions.

The brokerage wired $74,000 to a fraudulent account.

They filed a claim under their cyber policy, fully expecting coverage.

The surprise?

Their policy did NOT include social engineering or funds transfer fraud.

Cyber didn't pay.

Their bank didn't pay.

And the hacker disappeared with the money before sunrise.

The owner stared at the denial letter like it was written in another language. He thought "cyber" meant "everything digital."

It doesn't. Social engineering has to be added—every time.

Moral: Hackers don't break in—they trick their way in. And if your policy doesn't include social engineering, you're paying for the trick.

Who Needs Cyber Liability Insurance?

Short answer: Everyone.

If your business uses computers, email, stores customer data, processes payments, or has a website, you need Cyber Liability insurance.

The myth that "we're too small to be targeted" is exactly that—a myth. Small businesses are often easier targets because they have weaker security and less IT support.

You ESPECIALLY need it if you:
- Store customer payment information or personal data
- Handle protected health information (HIPAA compliance)
- Process credit card transactions
- Use email for business communications
- Store data in the cloud or on servers
- Have employees working remotely
- Accept wire transfers or ACH payments
- Rely on technology for daily operations

– In other words: if you run a business in 2025, you need Cyber Insurance.

The Most Common Cyber Threats (and Why You Need Coverage)

Ransomware

– Hackers encrypt your files and demand payment to unlock them. Average ransom demands range from $10,000 to $500,000+ for small businesses. Cyber Insurance covers negotiation, payment (if necessary), and system restoration.

Phishing Attacks

– Fake emails trick employees into clicking malicious links or sharing credentials. One click can compromise your entire network. Cyber Insurance covers the breach response and resulting damages.

Social Engineering (Business Email Compromise)

– Scammers impersonate vendors, executives, or clients to trick employees into wiring money or sharing sensitive data. These attacks are sophisticated and growing. Coverage must be specifically added to your policy.

Data Breaches

– Customer information is stolen—names, addresses, credit cards, Social Security numbers. You're legally required to notify affected individuals and often provide credit monitoring. Costs can easily exceed $100,000.

Denial of Service (DDoS) Attacks
- Hackers flood your website or systems with traffic, shutting you down. E-commerce businesses and online services are particularly vulnerable. Business interruption coverage helps cover lost revenue.

How Much Cyber Coverage Do You Need?

Cyber coverage limits typically range from $100,000 to $5 million, depending on your business size, industry, and data exposure.

Baseline recommendation:
- Small businesses (under 50 employees): $1 million minimum
- Mid-sized businesses (50-250 employees): $2-5 million
- Businesses handling sensitive data (healthcare, finance): $5 million+

Must-have endorsements:
- Social engineering/funds transfer fraud coverage
- Ransomware coverage with sufficient sublimits
- Business interruption with adequate waiting periods
- Regulatory defense and fines coverage

Cost factors:
- Industry (healthcare and finance pay more)
- Amount of sensitive data you handle
- Your cybersecurity measures (MFA, encryption, employee training)
- Annual revenue
- Claims history

- Typical costs: $1,000-$7,500/year for $1 million in coverage for small businesses. High-risk industries or larger limits cost significantly more.

What Carriers Require Before They'll Cover You

Cyber insurance underwriting has gotten stricter. Carriers want proof you're taking security seriously.

Common requirements:

- Multi-Factor Authentication (MFA) on all accounts
- Regular data backups (stored offline or in secure cloud)
- Endpoint detection and response (EDR) software
- Email filtering and spam protection
- Employee cybersecurity training
- Patch management and software updates
- Incident response plan

Warning: If you lie on your cyber application about your security controls and have a claim, the carrier can deny coverage. Be honest about your security posture.

The Bottom Line

Twenty years ago, cyber insurance didn't exist. Today, it's not optional—it's essential.

Cyber attacks aren't slowing down. They're getting more sophisticated, more frequent, and more expensive. The average cost of a data breach for a small business is over $200,000. Most small businesses can't survive that hit without insurance.

Your firewall, antivirus software, and IT team are your first line of defense. Cyber Liability Insurance is your last line of defense—and often the only thing standing between a cyber incident and business failure.

If you don't have Cyber Insurance yet, you're not just unprotected—you're gambling with your business's survival.

Next up: Chapter 7 will cover the Business Owners Policy (BOP)—the Swiss Army knife of small business insurance that bundles multiple coverages into one affordable package.

Chapter 7
BUSINESS OWNERS POLICY (BOP)
"The Swiss Army Knife of Small Business Insurance"

The Business Owners Policy—the BOP—is one of the best deals in commercial insurance. It bundles General Liability, Property, and Business Interruption coverage into one streamlined, affordable package designed specifically for small to mid-sized businesses.

For restaurants, retail shops, offices, service businesses, and countless other small operations, a BOP is often the foundation of their entire insurance program. It's cost-effective, comprehensive, and easier to manage than juggling multiple standalone policies.

But here's what most business owners don't realize: a BOP is powerful—but it's not a cure-all. It has gaps. It has limits. And if you don't understand what's covered and what's not, you can find yourself in serious trouble when you need it most.

In my 28 years, I've seen BOPs save businesses from catastrophe, and I've watched business owners learn the hard way that 'business owners policy' doesn't mean 'covers everything a business owner needs.'

Let me show you what I mean.

When a BOP SAVED a Small Business:

"One Spark Can Become a Storm—But the Right Shield Turns a Disaster Into a Detour"

A mom-and-pop print shop—forty years old, family run, the kind of place with dust on the shelves and loyalty in the air—had a late-night electrical fire. One overloaded outlet, one tired breaker, and in minutes the entire back room was swallowed in smoke.

But this little shop had something most don't: a Business Owner's Policy built the right way, not the cheap way.

Here's what hit them:
- Property coverage: paid for the fire damage, the equipment, the walls, the cleanup.
- Business interruption: carried them through three months of rebuilding, paying rent, payroll, and keeping the lights on when nothing was being printed.
- Liability: kicked in when smoke damage seeped into the next tenant's suite and they pointed the finger.
- The insurance check didn't just rebuild the shop. It rebuilt their hope.
- The hero moment? When the owner stood outside the charred doorway, shaking hands with the adjuster, and said with tears in his eyes: "If you hadn't made me upgrade this policy, we'd be gone."

That, my friend, is why BOPs matter.

What is a Business Owners Policy (BOP)?

A Business Owners Policy is a packaged insurance product that combines several essential coverages into one policy, specifically designed for small to mid-sized businesses.

Think of it as the commercial insurance equivalent of a homeowners policy—multiple protections bundled together at a lower price than buying each coverage separately.

Core coverages typically included in a BOP:
- General Liability: Covers bodily injury, property damage, personal injury, and advertising injury claims
- Commercial Property: Covers your building (if you own it), equipment, inventory, furniture, and fixtures
- Business Interruption (Business Income): Covers lost income and continuing expenses if your business is shut down due to a covered loss
- Extra Expense: Covers costs to continue operations after a covered loss (temporary location, equipment rental)

Common optional coverages (often available as endorsements):

- Equipment Breakdown (formerly Boiler & Machinery)
- Crime Coverage
- Employment Practices Liability (EPLI)
- Commercial Auto (sometimes)

– Inland Marine (for tools, equipment used off-premises)
– Sign coverage
– Outdoor property

When Someone Thought Their BOP Covered Something... But It DIDN'T:

"Assumptions Are the Most Expensive Coverage Gaps in the World"

A local tech repair shop—smart guy, good business, terrible attention span—bought a BOP online because it was the cheapest one he could click on.

Then came the storm.

A flash flood rolled through the shopping strip like a runaway ox. Water pushed under the door, crawled up the walls, soaked every tool, every part, every desktop, every laptop, every tablet waiting for repair. Thousands of dollars ruined.

He called the carrier, confident. He thought he was covered. He thought his BOP was a magic umbrella.

It wasn't.

No flood coverage. No equipment breakdown. No data restoration. No cyber. No spoilage. No nothing.

All he heard was the adjuster saying: "Unfortunately... this peril is excluded."

And that was that. $87,000 out of pocket. Half his inventory gone. A business never reopened.

His painful words: "I clicked the cheapest option because I thought all BOPs were the same."

A hard-earned truth: A BOP covers a lot—but it does NOT cover everything.

What BOPs Typically DON'T Cover (The Critical Gaps)

This is where business owners get into trouble. They assume their BOP is comprehensive protection, but there are significant exclusions and gaps.

Common exclusions and gaps in standard BOPs:

- Flood damage: Must be purchased separately through the National Flood Insurance Program (NFIP) or private market
- Earthquake damage: Requires separate coverage or endorsement
- Workers Compensation: NEVER included in a BOP—always a separate policy
- Professional Liability (E&O): Not covered—needs separate policy
- Cyber Liability: Not covered in standard BOPs (some carriers now offer it as an endorsement)
- Commercial Auto: Your business vehicles need separate commercial auto coverage
- Employee dishonesty/theft: May require crime coverage endorsement
- Pollution/environmental damage: Generally excluded
- Acts of war or terrorism: May be excluded or limited
- Intentional acts: Never covered

Critical point: Just because you have a BOP doesn't mean you're fully protected. You still need to identify gaps and add appropriate coverages.

The Common BOP SURPRISE That Hits Hard:

"Growth Without Updating Coverage Is Like Outgrowing Your Armor But Still Walking Into Battle"

A boutique candle shop had a fantastic year—new scents, online sales, booming holiday traffic. Inventory tripled. Revenue doubled. Exposure skyrocketed.

But her BOP? She hadn't touched it in three years.

Cue the fire marshal.

A small malfunction in her wax-melting equipment caused smoke damage and some charring. Not catastrophic... until the insurance adjuster pulled out the policy and recalculated values.

She was underinsured by nearly 50%. Coinsurance clause triggered like a mousetrap.

Instead of a $40,000 payout, she got just under $19,000. The rest? Straight from her savings.

Then came the second surprise: She thought her employees were covered for injuries. Nope—Workers Comp isn't part of a BOP.

The third surprise? She should've switched to a Commercial Package Policy two years earlier. Her revenue had outgrown the BOP eligibility and she didn't even know.

Her face said it all: "I didn't know success could hurt me."

But that's the quiet danger—a BOP is incredible...
UNTIL it no longer fits.

Who Qualifies for a BOP?

BOPs are designed for small to mid-sized businesses with
relatively straightforward operations. Not every business
qualifies.

Typical businesses that qualify for BOPs:

- Retail stores and shops
- Restaurants and food service (non-franchise, usually under $3M revenue)
- Office-based businesses (accounting, consulting, real estate)
- Service businesses (salons, repair shops, dry cleaners)
- Small manufacturing (depending on operations)
- Apartment buildings (typically under 6 stories)
- Warehouses and storage facilities

Eligibility is typically limited by:

- Building size (usually under 100,000 sq ft)
- Revenue (often capped at $3-10 million depending on carrier)
- Number of locations (many carriers limit to 3-5 locations)
- Industry/business type (high-hazard operations don't qualify)

Businesses typically NOT eligible for BOPs:

- Banks and financial institutions
- Auto dealerships and service stations

- Bars and nightclubs
- Large manufacturing operations
- Construction companies
- High-revenue or multi-location businesses (need Commercial Package Policy)

BOP vs. Commercial Package Policy (CPP): When to Upgrade

As your business grows, you may outgrow a BOP and need to switch to a Commercial Package Policy (CPP). A CPP is more customizable and designed for larger, more complex businesses.

Signs you've outgrown your BOP and need a CPP:

- Annual revenue exceeds $5-10 million
- Multiple locations (more than 3-5)
- Complex operations requiring specialized coverages
- Significant inventory or high-value equipment
- Your carrier says you no longer qualify for BOP pricing

A CPP offers more flexibility in coverage limits, endorsements, and terms—but it's typically more expensive than a BOP. The trade-off is worth it when you need the customization.

How Much Does a BOP Cost?

One of the biggest advantages of a BOP is cost efficiency. Because coverages are bundled, you typically pay 15-30% less than buying General Liability, Property, and Business Interruption separately.

Typical BOP costs (annual premium):
- Small retail shops: $500-$1,500
- Restaurants: $1,000-$3,000+
- Office businesses: $400-$1,200
- Service businesses: $500-$2,000
- Small manufacturing: $1,500-$5,000+

Pricing factors:
- Industry and business type
- Location (crime rates, natural disaster exposure)
- Building value and contents
- Revenue and payroll
- Claims history
- Coverage limits and deductibles
- Optional endorsements added

BOP Best Practices: How to Get the Most Protection

To maximize your BOP's value and avoid nasty surprises, follow these guidelines:

1. **Review and update annually**
   Your business changes—revenue grows, inventory increases, you add equipment or expand locations. Review your BOP every year and adjust limits to match your current exposure.

2. **Insure to full replacement cost, not actual cash value**
   Replacement cost coverage pays to rebuild or replace damaged property without depreciation. Actual cash value pays only depreciated value, leaving you short.

3. **Add Equipment Breakdown coverage**
   Standard property coverage doesn't cover mechanical or electrical breakdown. Equipment Breakdown endorsement covers HVAC systems, refrigeration, computers, and other critical equipment.

4. **Understand your Business Interruption limits**
   Most BOPs include 12 months of Business Interruption coverage, but some businesses need more. If rebuilding takes longer than expected, inadequate coverage leaves you paying expenses out of pocket.

5. **Don't assume—ask about exclusions**
   Every BOP is different. Read your policy or have your agent explain what's excluded. Flood? Earthquake? Cyber? Employee theft? Don't guess.

6. **Bundle additional coverages when possible**
   Many carriers allow you to add endorsements to your BOP for crime coverage, EPLI, cyber, and more. Bundling can save money and simplify management.

7. **Work with an agent who understands your industry**
   Not all BOPs are created equal, and not all agents understand the nuances of different industries. A knowledgeable agent will identify gaps you didn't know existed.

The Bottom Line

The Business Owners Policy is one of the smartest, most cost-effective insurance purchases a small business can make. It bundles essential coverages into one package at a price that's hard to beat.

But a BOP is not a silver bullet. It has gaps. It has limits. And if you don't review it regularly or understand what's excluded, you can find yourself facing financial disaster despite having insurance.

The print shop that survived the fire? They had the right BOP with the right limits. The tech shop that went under after the flood? They had the wrong BOP with the wrong assumptions. The candle shop that got hit with coinsurance penalties? They had a BOP that no longer fit their business.

A BOP is powerful—but only if it's built right, maintained properly, and supplemented where necessary.

Next up: Chapter 8 will cover Umbrella and Excess Liability— the extra layer of protection that kicks in when your primary policies aren't enough.

Chapter 8

UMBRELLA & EXCESS LIABILITY INSURANCE

"The Extra Layer That Protects Everything You've Built"

Umbrella and Excess Liability insurance is the coverage most business owners don't think about—until they desperately need it and don't have it.

It's the policy that sits quietly on top of your General Liability, Commercial Auto, and Employer's Liability coverage, waiting for the day when a catastrophic claim exceeds your primary policy limits. And when that day comes, it's the difference between surviving a lawsuit and losing everything.

Here's the thing about catastrophic claims: they're rare, but when they happen, they're devastating. A serious multi-vehicle accident. A customer permanently injured on your premises. A lawsuit with punitive damages that explodes past your $1 million general liability limit.

$1 million sounds like a lot of coverage—until a claim takes it in one bite and comes back for more.

In my 28 years, I've seen umbrella policies save businesses from bankruptcy, and I've watched business owners learn the hard way that 'adequate coverage' is only adequate until it isn't.

Let me show you what I mean.

The Day an Umbrella Policy SAVED a Business From Financial Ruin:

"When the Tide Rises Higher Than Your Walls,
You're Grateful for the Extra Sandbags"

A mid-sized HVAC contractor sent two techs to a routine service call. Nothing dramatic—just another Tuesday. On the way back, their company truck slid on a rain-slicked highway and caused a multi-vehicle pileup.

One SUV carried a family of four. Serious injuries. ICU. Long-term rehab. The kind of claim that unravels a business thread by thread.

Their commercial auto policy? $1 million liability limit.

The total claim? Just under $3.2 million.

That gap would've crushed them like a tin can—until the $5 million umbrella policy stepped in like a guardian angel with a checkbook.

It covered:
 – Excess bodily injury claims
 – Legal defense that ran into six figures
 – Settlement negotiations
 – Protection for the company AND the owner's personal assets

The hero moment came when the owner said: "I used to think umbrella was optional. After this... it's sacred."

Without that umbrella, Prestizia wouldn't be filing a renewal quote. They'd be filling out a business closure form.

Moral: Catastrophic claims don't announce themselves. Umbrella insurance is the safety net you pray you never need—and can't survive without when you do.

What is Umbrella & Excess Liability Insurance?

Umbrella and Excess Liability insurance provides an additional layer of liability protection that sits above your primary liability policies (General Liability, Commercial Auto, Employer's Liability).

When a claim exhausts the limits of your underlying policy, the umbrella kicks in to cover the excess—protecting your business assets and often your personal assets from catastrophic loss.

Umbrella vs. Excess Liability: What's the Difference?

The terms are often used interchangeably, but there's a technical difference:

- Umbrella Liability: Provides excess coverage AND may offer broader coverage than underlying policies. Can sometimes 'drop down' to fill gaps in underlying coverage (subject to a Self-Insured Retention).
- Excess Liability: Provides only excess coverage—it simply adds higher limits on top of your existing policies without broadening coverage. It's pure 'follow form' coverage.

- For most small to mid-sized businesses, 'Umbrella' and 'Excess' are functionally the same: extra limits when primary coverage runs out.

How Umbrella Coverage Works

Here's a simple example:
- Your General Liability policy has a $1 million limit per occurrence.
- You carry a $5 million Umbrella policy.
- A customer is seriously injured on your premises. The lawsuit settles for $3.8 million.

Here's how the coverage responds:
- General Liability pays: $1 million (its limit)
- Umbrella pays: $2.8 million (the excess above your primary limit)
- You pay: $0 (assuming no deductible or SIR applies)

Without the umbrella, you'd be personally liable for that $2.8 million gap.

When Someone DIDN'T Have Umbrella Coverage (or Didn't Have Enough):

"A Million Dollars Looks Enormous—
Until a Lawsuit Takes It in One Bite"

A local restaurant—family-owned, popular, always packed—had a simple slip-and-fall incident. A customer walked into the restroom, hit a wet floor, fractured their hip, and never fully recovered.

Medical bills piled up. Loss of income. Lifetime care projections. Add in punitive damages? The claim ballooned to $1.7 million.

Their general liability limit? $1 million.

No umbrella. No excess coverage. No backup plan.

The carrier paid its million and walked away. The remaining $700,000? Straight from the owner's savings, lines of credit, and the eventual sale of his business.

He told his agent afterward—too late—"I honestly thought $1M was the standard. I didn't know I needed more."

That misunderstanding cost him:
- His restaurant
- His retirement
- His peace of mind

A tough lesson: Umbrella coverage isn't for "big companies." It's for companies with something to lose.

What Umbrella/Excess Liability Typically Covers

Umbrella policies provide excess coverage over your underlying liability policies:

Coverage applies over:
- General Liability (bodily injury and property damage)
- Commercial Auto Liability
- Employer's Liability (the liability portion of Workers Comp)
- Certain other liability policies as scheduled

Umbrella typically covers:
- Bodily injury and property damage claims
- Personal injury (libel, slander, defamation)
- Advertising injury
- Legal defense costs (often in addition to policy limits)
- Worldwide coverage (usually)

Umbrella typically does NOT cover:
- Professional liability (E&O) claims
- Cyber liability claims
- Pollution or environmental damage
- Intentional acts or criminal conduct
- Contractual liability (depends on policy)
- Employment-related claims (discrimination, wrongful termination)
- Workers Compensation injuries (covered under WC, not umbrella)

Critical: Umbrella follows your underlying policies. If something isn't covered in your primary policy, it generally won't be covered by the umbrella either.

The Common Umbrella SURPRISE That Blindsides Business Owners:

"Coverage Only Works If the Ladders Line Up"

A tech consulting firm proudly carried a $2 million umbrella. They bragged about it, in fact. Thought they were ironclad.

Then came a lawsuit: A severe injury on their office stairs. Primary general liability paid its part. They expected the umbrella to handle the rest.

But the umbrella refused to attach.

Why? A few brutal surprises:

- Their underlying limits weren't high enough. Umbrella required $1M underlying, but their policy had only $500K.
- Certain exclusions were mirrored in the umbrella. If it's excluded down low, it's excluded up high—owners never knew.
- Aggregate was exhausted on the primary from a prior claim—umbrella wouldn't 'drop down.'
- Self-Insured Retention (SIR) added a $10,000 out-of-pocket they had no idea existed.
- The owner's exact words: "I didn't know an umbrella could still leave me standing in the rain."
- Most business owners believe: "Umbrella covers everything, right?"

Not quite. It follows the underlying like a shadow—and shadows disappear where the light is broken.

Key Terms You Need to Understand

Underlying Limits

These are the minimum liability limits your primary policies must carry for the umbrella to attach. Common requirements: $1 million General Liability, $1 million Auto Liability, $1 million Employer's Liability.

If your underlying limits are lower than required, the umbrella won't respond—or it will respond as if you carried the required limits, leaving you with a gap.

Self-Insured Retention (SIR)
This is essentially a deductible that applies when the umbrella 'drops down' to cover a claim not covered by an underlying policy. Typical SIRs range from $10,000 to $25,000.

Example: If your umbrella covers a claim that your primary policy excludes, you pay the SIR before the umbrella kicks in.

Follow Form vs. Standalone
Follow Form: The umbrella mirrors the terms, conditions, and exclusions of your underlying policies. If something is excluded below, it's excluded above.
Standalone: The umbrella has its own policy language and may provide broader coverage than the underlying. These are less common for small businesses.

Aggregate Limit
The maximum the umbrella will pay for all claims during the policy period. Once exhausted, coverage ends until the policy renews.

Example: A $5 million umbrella with a $5 million aggregate means you have $5 million total for the year—not $5 million per claim with unlimited claims.

How Much Umbrella Coverage Do You Need?
Umbrella coverage is typically sold in increments of $1 million. Common limits range from $1 million to $10 million for small to mid-sized businesses.

General guidelines:
- Small businesses (under 20 employees, low-risk operations): $1-2 million minimum
- Mid-sized businesses (20-100 employees, moderate risk): $2-5 million
- High-risk operations (construction, manufacturing, transportation): $5-10 million+
- Businesses with significant assets or high revenue: Match your umbrella limit to your net worth or annual revenue

Consider higher limits if:
- You have high annual revenue or significant business assets
- You own commercial real estate or valuable property
- Your business operates vehicles frequently
- You have public-facing operations (retail, restaurants, events)
- Contracts require specific umbrella limits
- You want to protect personal assets from business liability

How Much Does Umbrella Coverage Cost?

Umbrella insurance is remarkably affordable relative to the protection it provides.

Typical costs:
- $1 million umbrella: $200-$500/year
- $2 million umbrella: $350-$750/year
- $5 million umbrella: $750-$2,000/year
- $10 million umbrella: $1,500-$4,000/year

Pricing factors:
- Industry and business type
- Annual revenue and number of employees
- Underlying policy limits
- Claims history
- Amount of umbrella coverage purchased
- Whether you bundle with the same carrier as your primary policies

The value proposition: For $500-$2,000/year, you can protect everything you've built from a multi-million dollar catastrophic claim.

Umbrella Best Practices

1. **Match underlying limits to umbrella requirements**
   Don't assume your current limits are adequate. Check your umbrella's requirements and adjust your primary policies accordingly.
2. **Bundle when possible**
   Buying your umbrella from the same carrier as your primary policies often results in better pricing and smoother claims handling.
3. **Review coverage annually as your business grows**
   As your revenue, assets, and exposure increase, your umbrella limits should increase too.
4. **Understand the SIR**
   Know what your Self-Insured Retention is and budget for it. It's not huge, but it can be a surprise if you're not expecting it.

5. **Don't skip umbrella to save money**

   Umbrella coverage is one of the best insurance values available. Cutting it to save a few hundred dollars a year is a catastrophic gamble.

The Bottom Line

Umbrella and Excess Liability insurance is the coverage you hope you never use—but absolutely cannot afford to be without.

The HVAC contractor who walked away from a $3.2 million claim? That umbrella policy saved his business, his livelihood, and probably his marriage. The restaurant owner who faced a $1.7 million slip-and-fall? He lost everything because he thought $1 million was enough.

Catastrophic claims are rare. But when they happen, they're business-ending. Your primary liability policies protect you from everyday risks. Your umbrella protects you from the nightmare scenarios that blow through your primary limits and come for everything else.

For a few hundred to a few thousand dollars a year, you can protect everything you've spent years building. That's not optional coverage—that's essential survival insurance.

Next up: Chapter 9 will cover Employment Practices Liability Insurance (EPLI)—the coverage that protects you when employees sue for wrongful termination, discrimination, or harassment.

CHAPTER 9
EMPLOYMENT PRACTICES LIABILITY INSURANCE (EPLI)

"When Your Employees Become Your Biggest Risk"

Employment Practices Liability Insurance—EPLI—is the coverage most small business owners don't think they need until an employee walks into an attorney's office with a termination letter and a grudge.

Wrongful termination. Discrimination. Harassment. Retaliation. Hostile work environment. Wage and hour disputes. These aren't just problems for Fortune 500 companies—they're lurking in every business with employees, from two-person startups to 200-person operations.

Here's the reality: you can do everything right as an employer—follow the rules, document performance issues, treat people fairly—and still get sued. Because employment lawsuits aren't always about what you did. Sometimes they're about what an employee claims you did, and proving your innocence costs a fortune.

In my 28 years, I've seen EPLI coverage save businesses from financial ruin, and I've watched business owners without coverage drain their savings defending themselves against claims that were eventually dismissed. Even when you win, you lose—unless you have EPLI.

Let me show you why this coverage matters.

When EPLI Coverage SAVED a Business From an Employment Lawsuit:

"One Accusation Can Burn Hotter Than Any Fire. The Right Coverage Is the Water That Keeps the Flames From Eating Your World"

A small manufacturing company—tight-knit crew, family atmosphere, "we're all friends here"—terminated an employee for chronic absenteeism.

The employee didn't take it well.

He lawyered up and filed a claim: Wrongful termination + retaliation + discrimination.

Suddenly that "friendly workplace" turned into a court battlefield.

But this business had something most don't: EPLI coverage tucked quietly into their policy stack.

Here's what it covered:
- Attorney fees
- Discovery costs
- Mediation
- Settlement negotiations
- A final settlement that would've knocked the business out cold
- Total claim: $185,000
- Business out-of-pocket: $5,000 retention

The hero moment? When the owner said with shaking hands: "If we didn't have this, they'd be auctioning off my equipment."

EPLI didn't just save the business. It saved the owner from losing his peace, his livelihood, and his future.

What is Employment Practices Liability Insurance (EPLI)?

EPLI is insurance that protects businesses against claims made by employees (current, former, or prospective) alleging employment-related wrongdoing.

It covers the legal defense costs, settlements, and judgments associated with employment practices claims—even if the allegations are groundless.

EPLI typically covers claims for:
- Wrongful termination or discharge
- Discrimination (age, race, gender, disability, religion, etc.)
- Sexual harassment or hostile work environment
- Retaliation (firing someone for whistleblowing or filing a complaint)
- Failure to promote or hire
- Wrongful discipline or demotion
- Breach of employment contract
- Negligent evaluation or retention
- Invasion of privacy
- Defamation or emotional distress

EPLI typically does NOT cover:
- Bodily injury or property damage (that's General Liability)
- Workers Compensation claims (workplace injuries)
- Wage and hour claims (often excluded or require separate endorsement)
- Violations of OSHA, ADA, FMLA (may require endorsements)
- Intentional violations of employment law
- Criminal acts
- Claims by independent contractors (unless third-party coverage added)

When Someone DIDN'T Have EPLI Coverage:

*"In the Court of Employment Law,
Innocence Still Costs a Fortune"*

A boutique retail store fired an employee for repeated no-calls and no-shows. Nothing dramatic... they thought.

Two months later, the owner was served papers. The employee claimed:
- Hostile work environment
- Harassment
- Wrongful termination
- Emotional distress

Even though the claims were exaggerated, twisted, and in some places outright fabricated, here's the brutal truth:

Defense is expensive even when you win.

Legal fees reached $92,000 before they even stepped into mediation. The case settled for another $60,000. No EPLI. No safety net. No mercy.

To cover the cost, the owner:
- Drained personal savings
- Sold inventory at a loss
- Shut down one location
- Took out a loan that took years to recover from

Her words still sting: "I thought lawsuits happened to big companies... not to me."

But lawsuits don't hunt size. They hunt opportunity.

The Cost Reality of Employment Lawsuits
Employment lawsuits are expensive—win or lose. Here's what defending yourself typically costs:

Average defense costs (without EPLI):
- Employment attorney retainer: $5,000-$15,000 upfront
- Total legal fees (through trial): $75,000-$200,000+
- Average settlement (if you settle): $40,000-$125,000
- Jury awards (if you lose at trial): $150,000-$500,000+
- Time and emotional toll: Immeasurable

Sobering fact: Even if you win the case, you still pay your legal fees. A frivolous lawsuit you successfully defend can still cost $100,000+.

The Common EPLI SURPRISE That Catches Owners Off Guard:

"Employment Law Is a Minefield. Stepping Lightly Doesn't Keep You From Being Blown Up"

One consulting firm thought they were covered in every direction. They had GL. They had WC. They had a solid BOP. They thought they were bulletproof.

Then came the storm.

A freelance contractor accused one of their employees of third-party harassment. Not an employee. Not on payroll. Not technically 'theirs.'

But the claim was filed anyway. And the business owner discovered:

- General liability doesn't cover employment-related claims.
- EPLI doesn't automatically cover third-party claims unless endorsed.
- Independent contractors can sue for discrimination or harassment.
- Wage and hour disputes often have limited EPLI protection (or none without specific endorsements).
- Prior acts exclusions can wipe out coverage for anything that started before the policy date.
- Defense-costs-within-limits means the legal fees eat up the pot before the settlement even hits.

The owner's exact stunned words: "I truly didn't know ANY of this."

That's the problem. Business owners assume. Policies exclude. And claims don't care.

Who Needs EPLI?

Short answer: Every business with employees.

It doesn't matter if you have 2 employees or 200. If you have people on payroll, you have employment practices exposure.

You ESPECIALLY need EPLI if:
- You've had employee turnover (especially terminations)
- You're growing and hiring regularly
- You have managers or supervisors who make employment decisions
- You operate in high-litigation states (California, New York, Texas, Florida)
- You don't have a dedicated HR department
- Your employee handbook is outdated (or non-existent)
- You use independent contractors regularly
- Your business has public-facing operations

Myth: "We treat our employees well, so we don't need EPLI."
Reality: Employment lawsuits aren't always about actual wrongdoing. They're often about perception, miscommunication, or opportunistic employees who see a payday. Even the best employers get sued.

Key EPLI Coverage Features to Understand

Defense Costs: Included vs. In Addition to Limits

Defense costs included (within limits): Legal fees and settlements both come out of the same policy limit. If you have a $1 million policy and spend $300K on defense, you only have $700K left for settlement.

Defense costs in addition to limits: Legal fees are paid separately, and the policy limit is reserved entirely for settlements/judgments. This is more expensive but provides better protection.

Recommendation: Pay extra for 'defense in addition to limits' if you can. Legal fees can eat up your entire policy limit.

Prior Acts Coverage vs. Claims-Made

Most EPLI policies are claims-made, meaning the claim must be made during the policy period, not when the alleged wrongdoing occurred.

Prior acts coverage (or full prior acts date) covers employment actions that occurred before your policy started, as long as the claim is made during the policy period.

Critical: When buying EPLI for the first time or switching carriers, make sure you have full prior acts coverage. Otherwise, you're not covered for anything that happened before the policy start date.

Third-Party Coverage
- Standard EPLI covers claims by employees. Third-party coverage extends protection to claims by

non-employees: customers, vendors, independent contractors, clients.
  - Example: A customer alleges harassment by one of your employees. Without third-party coverage, your EPLI won't respond.

Wage and Hour Coverage
  - Many EPLI policies exclude wage and hour claims (unpaid overtime, misclassification, meal/rest break violations) or offer it as an optional endorsement.
  - Wage and hour claims are increasingly common and expensive. If your policy doesn't include this coverage, add it.

How Much EPLI Coverage Do You Need?

EPLI limits typically range from $500,000 to $5 million, depending on business size and risk.

General guidelines:
  - Small businesses (1-20 employees): $500,000–$1 million
  - Mid-sized businesses (20-100 employees): $1-2 million
  - Larger businesses (100+ employees): $2-5 million
  - High-risk industries or rapid growth: Higher limits

Consider higher limits if:
  - You've had prior employment claims or lawsuits
  - You operate in high-litigation states
  - You're hiring or terminating employees frequently
  - Your managers aren't trained in employment law
  - You don't have strong HR policies and documentation

How Much Does EPLI Cost?

EPLI premiums are based on number of employees, industry, claims history, and state.

Typical costs:
- Small businesses (1-10 employees): $500-$1,500/year
- Mid-sized businesses (10-50 employees): $1,500-$5,000/year
- Larger businesses (50-100 employees): $5,000-$15,000/year
- 100+ employees: $15,000-$50,000+/year

Pricing factors:
- Number of employees
- Industry (hospitality and retail pay more)
- State (California, New York have higher rates)
- Claims history
- Employee turnover rate
- HR practices and training programs
- Policy limits and deductible/retention

EPLI Best Practices: How to Minimize Risk

EPLI coverage is essential, but the best protection is preventing claims in the first place.

1. **Create and maintain an updated employee handbook**
   Clear policies on harassment, discrimination, termination procedures, and complaint processes are your first line of defense.

2. **Train managers and supervisors**

Most employment lawsuits stem from poor management decisions. Train your supervisors on employment law basics.

3. **Document everything**

   Performance reviews, disciplinary actions, warnings, and termination reasons should all be documented in writing.

4. **Use consistent termination procedures**

   Treat all employees the same way. Inconsistent treatment is a fast track to discrimination claims.

5. **Investigate complaints immediately**

   When an employee raises a harassment or discrimination complaint, take it seriously and investigate promptly.

6. **Work with HR professionals or employment attorneys**

   Before terminating an employee (especially for cause), consult with an HR professional or employment attorney.

7. **Buy EPLI coverage before you need it**

   EPLI is claims-made coverage. If you wait until you have a problem, it's too late.

The Bottom Line

Employment Practices Liability Insurance isn't optional in today's litigious environment—it's essential survival insurance.

The manufacturing company that faced a $185,000 wrongful termination claim? EPLI saved them. The retail store owner who defended a frivolous lawsuit for $152,000 out of pocket? No EPLI destroyed her. The consulting firm blindsided by third-party harassment claims? They learned the hard way that assumptions about coverage are expensive.

You can be the best employer in the world—fair, kind, generous—and still get sued. Because employment lawsuits aren't always about what you did. They're about what someone claims you did, and proving your innocence costs a fortune.

If you have employees, you have employment practices exposure. And if you don't have EPLI, you're one disgruntled employee away from financial catastrophe.

Next up: Chapter 10 will tie everything together—your comprehensive action plan for building a complete, intelligent insurance program that protects your business from every angle.

Chapter 10

PUTTING IT ALL TOGETHER

"Your Complete Business Protection Strategy"

You've just walked through nine chapters of real-world insurance stories—the saves, the disasters, and the surprises that catch business owners off guard.

You've seen what happens when coverage works, and what happens when it doesn't. You've learned the difference between having insurance and having the RIGHT insurance.

Now it's time to put it all together and build a comprehensive protection strategy for YOUR business.

This final chapter gives you the tools, checklists, and action steps to ensure your business is protected from every angle—so you can focus on growing your business instead of worrying about what could go wrong.

Quick Recap: The 9 Essential Coverages Every Business Should Know

1. **General Liability**
   Your first line of defense against bodily injury, property damage, and everyday business risks.

2. **Property Insurance**
   Protects your building, contents, equipment, and inventory from fire, theft, storms, and more.

3. **Commercial Auto**
   Covers company vehicles, employees driving for work, and hired/non-owned exposures.

4. **Workers Compensation**
   Medical bills, lost wages, and protection from employee injury lawsuits.

5. **Professional Liability (E&O)**
   Protects against mistakes, errors, missed deadlines, and service-related claims.

6. **Cyber Liability**
   Protects against data breaches, ransomware, cyberattacks, and the cost of restoring operations.

7. **Business Owners Policy (BOP)**
   A powerful bundle—property + liability + business interruption—for small to mid-sized businesses.

8. **Commercial Umbrella**
   An extra layer of liability protection when claims exceed standard policy limits.

9. **Employment Practices Liability (EPLI)**
   Covers lawsuits related to hiring, firing, discrimination, harassment, and workplace behavior.

Nine coverages. One protection strategy. When they work together, they keep your business standing tall—even in the fiercest storm.

The Complete Business Insurance Checklist

A simple, powerful list every business should review yearly.

- Do you have general liability?
- Do you have property coverage or a BOP?
- Do you insure your equipment and inventory properly?
- Do you have commercial auto (or hired/non-owned)?
- Do you have workers comp (even if not required)?
- Do you carry a commercial umbrella?
- Do you have cyber and EPLI?
- Do you have professional liability?
- Are your limits high enough for today's risks?
- Is your revenue, payroll, or property updated on your policy?
- Are your certificates and endorsements correct?
- Do you know your exclusions?

If any box gives you pause—it's time for a review.

Coverage Gaps Assessment

The silent dangers most business owners never notice.

Here are the most common hidden gaps:

- Outdated property values
- No cyber
- No EPLI
- No umbrella
- Vehicles not listed correctly
- Employees using personal cars for business

- No coverage for subcontractors
- Missing endorsements for your industry
- Lapsed COIs
- Inventory increases not updated
- New equipment not added
- Old limits that haven't kept up with inflation

A good agent finds these. A great agent fixes them before they cost you everything.

Industry-Specific Recommendations

Different industries face different threats. Here's what matters most by category:
- Contractors & Trades
- Tools & equipment
- Inland marine
- Workers comp
- Contractors E&O
- Auto & umbrella
- Retail & Storefronts
- BOP with business interruption
- Cyber
- Money & securities
- Spoilage (if needed)
- EPLI
- Restaurants & Food Service
- Liquor liability
- Foodborne illness
- Equipment breakdown

- Business income with extra expense
- Professional Services (Consultants, Agents, Advisors)
- E&O
- Cyber
- EPLI
- HNOA (if traveling to clients)
- Home-Based Businesses
- Homeowners does NOT cover business
- BOP or home-based business rider
- Liability for clients visiting your home

Every industry has its own fingerprint—and its own vulnerabilities.

The Annual Review Process

Because your business grows, stretches, and changes—your coverage should too.

Review your policies when:
- Your renewal is coming up
- You purchase new equipment
- You add or reduce staff
- Your revenue changes significantly
- You add a new location
- You sign a new contract requiring specific limits
- You start offering new services
- You change vehicles
- You take on larger jobs

A yearly insurance checkup is like a doctor's visit—it keeps the whole system healthy.

Red Flags You're Underinsured

If any of these apply, danger is near:
- Your limits haven't changed in 3+ years
- Your business has grown but your coverage hasn't
- You don't know what your policy excludes
- You don't have cyber or EPLI
- You don't have an umbrella
- You bought the cheapest policy you could find online
- You never meet with your agent
- You haven't had a professional review in 12 months

These aren't small flags—they're flashing lights on the dashboard.

Why You Need a Trusted Advisor (Not Just a Policy)

Insurance isn't paperwork. It's protection.

And protection only works when someone who understands your risk is steering the ship.

A trusted advisor:
- Explains what you truly need
- Spots gaps before lawsuits do
- Understands your industry
- Keeps your policy updated
- Stands with you when claims hit
- Helps you build long-term protection, not short-term price shopping

This is where Prestizia Insurance stands apart.

We don't sell policies—we build shields.

Your Next Step—The Call to Action

- You've read the stories.
- You've seen the risks.
- Now it's time to strengthen your business.

*SCHEDULE YOUR FREE BUSINESS INSURANCE PROTECTION REVIEW

A full, no-pressure assessment to uncover gaps, strengthen coverage, and give you peace of mind.

*Optional Next Steps
- Download the Coverage Gap Checklist
- Request a custom quote
- Ask for a full risk review
- Update your current policies
- Join The Protection Circle at TheProtectionCircle.com

Your business deserves a shield—not a guess.

Contact Information—Prestizia Insurance
Prestizia Insurance
Phone: 972-854-7784
Email: service@prestiziainsurance.com
Website: PrestiziaInsurance.com
The Protection Circle: TheProtectionCircle.com
Office Address:
6060 N Central Expy, Ste 500
Dallas, TX 75206
Instagram: @GoPrestizia

Facebook: @GoPrestizia
Twitter/X: @GoPrestizia
TikTok: @GoPrestizia
YouTube: @GoPrestizia

Connect With Us on Social Media:

A Final Word

In 28 years of working with businesses across every industry, I've learned one truth that never changes:

The businesses that survive aren't always the biggest or the most profitable—they're the ones that are protected.

Fires happen. Lawsuits happen. Cyber attacks happen. Employees sue. Customers slip and fall. Equipment breaks. Accidents occur.

The difference between a devastating loss and a manageable claim is having the right coverage, with the right limits, reviewed by someone who actually understands your business.

This book gave you the knowledge. Now it's time to take action.

Reach out to Prestizia Insurance. Let's review your coverage together. Let's find the gaps. Let's build you a shield that actually works.

Because your business deserves more than a policy—it deserves protection.

—John Crist
President, Prestizia Insurance
Dallas-Fort Worth, Texas